HAWAII'S
SEEDS
and
SEED LEIS

AN
IDENTIFICATION
GUIDE

Laurie Shimizu Ide

MUTUAL PUBLISHING

Library of Congress Catalog Card
Number: 00-107410

First Printing, November 2000
1 2 3 4 5 6 7 8 9

Design by Angela Wu-Ki Design and Julie Matsuo
Cover Design by Julie Matsuo

ISBN 1-56647-338-1

Mutual Publishing
1215 Center Street, Suite 210
Honolulu, Hawaii 96816
Ph: (808) 732-1709
Fax: (808) 734-4094
e-mail: mutual@lava.net
www.mutualpublishing.com

Printed in Korea

Mahalo Nui Loa

I am deeply grateful to the following individuals who unselfishly gave their time, energy and knowledge to make this book possible:

Toshi and Ethel Shimizu

Elaine Mezurashi

Barney Bareng

Yukio and Audrey Toguchi

Richard and Trudy Aloiau

Helen M. Chamizo

Terry M. Pacheco

Tim Helton

Leihulu M. Greene

Patricia K. McGuire

John and Doreen Saito

David Chock

Dana Pascal

Diane English

Linda L. Grass

Heidi Leianuenue Bornhorst

The Staff at Photo Trends

Howard Hamada

Louis Ko Ohana

Special appreciation to my husband Karl,

for his patience, support and technical advice.

Table of Contents

PREFACE

Hawai'i has so many beautiful seeds. They offer endless possi-
bilities for a crafter working in traditional styles, or someone
with an inventive edge. The purpose of this book is to introduce
hobbyists as well as those with a general interest to the great
variety of decorative seeds in the islands. Included here are
native plants and many others that have been introduced in the
last two hundred years. They add up to an extraordinary mix-
ture of sizes, shapes and colors. Correctly identifying each is
very important, and safety is emphasized for toxic varieties.
This guide should make gathering and using these wonderful
seeds a real pleasure.

*P*lants are arranged in alphabetical order by their common names as used in Hawai'i. The islands being so international, however, and the plants being so international as well, there are often many familiar names for the same plant. I selected what I felt were the most popular. It seemed best to include quite a variety because sometimes a name refers to the flower, or its vine, or its seed, or a combination of these. Sometimes you will find a phonetic translation of a "Hawaiianized" name. The scientific Latin term—standard for botanists all over the world—is also given, but here in the islands the average crafter is likely to use a common name like "wood rose" or "blue marble."

Introduction

Throughout Hawai'i's history, its people used all sorts of natural materials for adornment. A lei was made of flowers, shells, feathers and/or seeds. Today this tradition continues to thrive, and part of living here is dressing "island style." This means aloha attire, which is always beautifully complemented by a lei.

Seed leis are worn by men, women and children. They are used as necklaces, head- and hatbands, bracelets and anklets for hula dancers, and are a beloved craft practiced by young and old. As a gift from nature, seeds can be gathered easily and without harming the environment. Using and wearing them also increases awareness of our natural world and its resources. Seeds are "nature's beads," and they connect us to a cultural craft that keeps our islands' aloha spirit alive.

A seed lei may actually consist of seeds, nuts, beans, cones, and the shells of seeds. With the modern use of the drill and drill press, innovative styles are constantly being created. Drilling and stringing seeds at different angles or in different combinations makes for new, unique patterns. This kind of creativity is truly a rewarding experience. For the beginner, however, a few basic rules are important. Certain seeds or parts of seeds can be highly toxic. They must be treated with caution even if they're beautiful or look delicious. Toxicity ranges from zero to mild to fatal.

Safety Tips:
1. Research the plant and seed before beginning a project.
2. DO NOT eat any part of the seed or plant.
3. Wash hands after handling the seed or plant.
4. Keep unsupervised children from contact with the
   seed and plant.

A novice should probably avoid collecting or using the seeds known as "be-still," and "black-eyed susan." Skilled, professional craftspeople work with these seeds, and know that both are toxic if digested, or if some of the seed enters the body through a cut, a sore, or contact with the eyes. A lei of either of these seeds is also worn over clothing to prevent a mix of perspiration and any toxic substance. (The "castor bean" lei has been excluded from this book because of the high risk involved in working with it.) But warnings aside, you will find that most seeds are people-friendly.

A few other pointers are important. Enjoy yourself when collecting the seeds, but take care and observe the tradition of respecting harmony in nature. Pick up only what you need. Leave seeds for others, and for the species to survive. Do not break branches or harm the plant. Preserve it for future generations. If you grow your own non-native species, keep them from spreading beyond a controlled boundary at the expense of our unique native plants.

Once you have made a lei, proper storage is also important. Nature intends for seeds to sprout. Those that don't are eaten by insects or decompose back into the earth. So keep your seed lei in a sealed plastic bag in the refrigerator. Take it out about an hour prior to wearing, then refrigerate it after use. Freezing a lei in a sealed plastic container works as well. Take it out one day prior to use, and freeze it again afterwards. Another method of stopping bug damage is to put mothballs in a separate, unsealed plastic bag along with your lei and store both in a cool area. Air out your seed lei one day prior to wearing. Or wrap it in dry tobacco or bay leaves, put it in a sealed plastic container, and store in a cool area. If the seeds in your lei are hollow or have no contents, though, it can be displayed on a wall or shelf in your home.

If you're a beginner, a good candidate to start with is the kukui, or candlenut. Its shell is very hard and polishes beautifully. The husk and meat are both benign and even have medicinal uses. The kukui also comes from a richly traditional tree that is sited in many ancient legends and songs.

I hope you will find this book just the beginning to designing beautiful seed-lei jewelry. Perhaps the various examples in ***Hawai'i's Seeds and Seed Lei: An Identification Guide*** will lend you inspiration as well.

ALEXANDRIAN LAUREL
—*Calophyllum inophyllum*
Kamani, Punnai Nut, True Kamani

- Mangosteen Family (*Clusiaceae*)

- A low branching tree, to 60 feet tall. Leaves are shiny, blunt, oblong, 3-8 inches long.

- Flowers are white, in clusters, fragrant when fresh.

- Fruits are green, globose, 1-1/2 inch in diameter turning yellowish when dried.

BALLOON VINE

—*Cardiospermum halicaccabum*

Pōniu, 'Inalua, Heart Seed

Photo by Gerald D. Carr

- (Synonym: C. Microcarpum by authors)

- Soapberry Family (*Sapindaceae*)

- A slender stemmed vine up to 10 feet high. Leaves are three-parted, 2 to 4 inches long.

- Flowers are white, small, irregular-shaped, borne together on slender stems at leaf axils.

- Fruits are brown, thin-shelled, winged, inflated, ovoid capsule, 1 inch in diameter, containing 3 round black seeds, 1/4 inches in diameter, with a white heart scar.

BE-STILL

—Thevetia puruviana
Noho-maile, Yellow Oleander,
Lucky Bean, Lucky Nut, Trumpet Flower

- Periwinkle Family
(*Apocynaceae*)

- A low branching small
tree. Leaves are shiny, 3
to 6 inches long, 1/4 inch
wide.

- Flowers are bright to
golden yellow, funnel-
shaped, mild fragrance,
clustered at branch tips.

- Mature fruits are black, shiny, about 1-1/2 inches in
diameter, containing 2 triangular, split seeds. All parts
of this plant are very poisionous if digested.

BLACK-EYED SUSAN

—*Arbus precatorius*

Pūkiawe, Rosary Pea, Bead Vine, Prayer Vine

Photo by Murray Fagg ©Australian National Botanic Gardens

- Pea Family (*Fabaceae*)

- A slender, branching vine up to 25 feet long. Leaves have 7 to 12 pairs of thin, oblong leaflets, each about 1/2 inch long.

- Flowers are pink or lavender in clusters. The seed pods are in clusters, containing bright red, oval seeds with a black patch.

- The seeds contain abrin, a poision destroyed by heat. Seeds are extremely toxic if digested.

Lei from the collection of Louis Ko Ohana

BLUE MARBLE

—*Elaeocarpus grandis*
Māpala Polū, Blue Fig, Quandong

- Linden Family (*Tiliaceae*)

- A tall tree, with smooth, narrow leaves, 4 to 8 inches long, sometimes changing from green to red before falling.

- Flowers are whitish, with fringed edges and many stamens.

- The mature fruits are bright blue, containing a round, deeply wrinkled, four-seeded, brown stone.

CALABASH

—Crescentia cujete

La'amia

- Bignonia Family (*Bignoniaceae*)

- A low tree, long spreading or drooping branches. Leaves are arranged spirally on the branches, 2 to 6 inches long.

- Flowers are chartreuse with purple markings, irregularly bell-shaped, usually solitary on branches, opening mainly at night, unpleasant smelling.

- Mature fruits are yellow which turn to brown, round, 5 to 12 inches in diameter, hard- shelled, containing pulp and many small seeds.

CANAVALIA

—Canavalia cathartica

Ture Mauna-loa, Mauna-loa, Kauhi

- (Synonym: C. microcarpa, C. turdida, C. ensiformis by authors)

- Pea Family (*Fabaceae*)

- A fast-growing vine. Leaves are broad-ovate, pointed, 3 to 6 inches long.

- Flowers are pink or lavender, 1 to 1-1/2 inch long, pea-like, light fragrance.

- The seed pods are thick, having about six, oval, flat, brown to black seeds.

CANDLENUT

—*Aleurites moluccana*
Kukui

- Spruge Family (*Euphorbiaceae*)

- A tree having angularly pointed, silvery, pale-green leaves with whitish down covering.

- Flowers are small, whitish, arranged in clusters, mild fragrance.

- Fruits are green, about 2 inches in diameter, roundish to heart-shaped, containing 1 to 2 nuts ranging from white, brown, whitish-brown to black.

CANNA LILY

—*Canna indica*

Ali'ipoe, Li'ipoe, Poloka, Canna Indian Shot

- **Canna Family (*Cannaceae*)**

- **A plant about 2 to 5 feet tall, rising from a large root, having a slender stem. Leaves are oval, narrow, about 6 to 20 inches long.**

- **Flowers may vary in color due to the crossing of many species.**

- **Pods are 1 inch long, erect, dried, three-parted, containing small, black, round seeds.**

Lei from the collection of Louis Ko Ohana

CHINESE LANTERN
—*Hernandia Nymphaeifolia*
Kukui Hele Pō Kina, Jack in the Box

- (Synonyms: H. ovigera, H. peltata, H. sonora by authors)

- Hernandia Family (*Hernandiaceae*)

- A tall, evergreen with a wide trunk and branches. Leaves shiny, broadly ovate to 8 inches long, curled up.

- Flowers are greenish yellow, small in clusers at branch tips.

- The fruits are clustered, red, hollow, 2 inches in diameter, flat, with a large opening at the bottom, containing a black nut.

CORAL TREE (COMMON)

—*Erythrina crista-galli*

Wiliwili Haole, Coral Tree

- Pea Family (*Fabaceae*)

- A shrubby tree. Leaves are shiny, with three smooth, oval leaflets.

- Flowers are rich dark red, oblong, near branch ends, about 2 inches long.

- Seeds are dark brown with light markings in a swollen, curved pod.

CORAL TREE (INDIAN AND HAWAIIAN) OR TIGERS CLAW

—*Erythrina variegata*

Wiliwili Haole, (Blackish Seed, White Seed, Dark Pink Seed)

—*Erythrina sandwicensis*

Native Hawaiian Wiliwili, (Red Seed)

- Pea Family (*Fabaceae*)

- A medium to large-sized low-land tree, having thick branches with short, black thorns. Leaves are 4 to 6 inches long, with three broad triangular leaflets, which fall in January and February.

- Flowers are in clusters at branch ends, ranging in colors from dark-red, orange, green, and white.

- Seeds range in colors from back, dark purple, dark pink with black markings, white and the Native Hawaiian Sandwicensis, red.

CORDIA

—Cordia Subcordata
Kou

- **Borage Family** (*Boraginaceae*)

- **A tree up to 30 feet high, having a wide-spreading crown, and a pale grey, grooved, flaky bark. Leaves are oval, curled up, pointed at tip and rounded at base.**

- **Flowers are orange, scentless, about 1 inch long, 1 1/2 inches in diameter, in clusters on branch ends.**

- **The dried fruits are round, about 1 inch in diameter, containing a triangular-shaped, grooved stone, with one to four seeds.**

CYCAD

—*Cycas circinalis*
Keko, Sago Palm

- Cycas Family (*Cycadaceae*)

- A palm-like, short tree, with a wide trunk. Leaves are fern-like, curving down, smooth, having many pointed, narrow leaflets.

- Male and female flowers develop on separate trees. Male trees produce erect brown cones, while female trees produce wooly, indented modified leaves which bare 6 to 10 seeds at leaf ends.

- The mature fruits are orange, inside is a large oval nut-like seed with a kernel that is very toxic if digested.

ELEPHANTS EAR

—Enterolobium cyclocarpum

Pepeiao 'Elepane, Earpod, Ear Seed

- Mimosa Subfamily (*Mimosoideae*)

- A tall, wide-canopied tree, with a large grey trunk and branches. Leaves are diciduous and twice divided, having four to nine pairs of pinnae, each pinna having 10 to 30 pairs of leaflets.

- Flowers are white, round, about 1 inch in diameter. Seed pods are dark brown, shiny, circular, flat, about 3 to 4 inches in diameter, resembling an "elephant's ear," containing many dark brown seeds with an oval marking.

GREY NICKERS

—Caesalpina Bonduc
Kakalaioa, Hawaiian Grey Pearl, Hawaiian Pearl, Captain Rose

Photo by W. Arthur Whistler

- (Synonym: C. bonducella, C. major, C. crista by authors)

- Pea Family (*Fabaceae*)

- A large, weedy, prickly shrub that climbs or straggles in dry low lands. The numerous paired leaflets are oblong to round, 1/2 to 2 inches long, having prickles on leaf stems.

- Flowers are small, yellow, in crowded racemes.

- Mature pods are brown, prickly, oblong, containing two or three grey, oval seeds.

IRONWOOD

—Casuarina equisetifolia

Pa'ina, She Oak, Warrior Tree, Beefwood Oak, Toa

- Casuarina Family (*Casuarinaceae*)

- A tall, slender, drooping tree, up to150 feet, having a greyish, furrowed bark.

- The seeding and pollen-bearing flowers are separate on the same tree. The pollen bearing flowers form long, brown cylinders slightly larger than the needles; the seeding flowers appear at the base of the needles as small reddish tufts.

- Mature cones are brown, round to oval, about 3/4 inch long, flattened at both ends, having hardened bracts, each containing a flat, one-winged seed.

JAVA ALMOND
—*Canarium vulgare*
Pili, Pili-nut, Kenari-nut

- Torchwood Family (*Burseraceae*)

- A tall tree with a grey bark. Leaves are about 12 inches long, having 3 to 5 pairs of oval leaflets, an extra leaf at the end.

- Flowers are small, yellowish-white, three-parted.

- The fruits are oval, blackish blue, about 2 inches long, containing a three-sided nut.

JAVA OLIVE
—Sterculia foetida
'Oliwa lāwa, Skunk Tree, Kelumpang, Bangar

- Cocoa Family (*Sterculiaceae*)

- A large, deciduous tree. Leaves are shinny, about 12 inches wide, having 5 to 11 oval, pointed leaflets.

- Flowers are red and yellow, or purple, having an unpleasant odor.

- The fruit has one to five scarlet, smooth, rounded sections, each about 3 inches in diameter, splitting open when mature to reveal 10 to 15 grey, oblong seeds an inch long.

JOB'S TEARS
—*Coix lacryma jobi*
Pū'ohe'ohe, Panyas Beads

- **Grass Family (*Gramineae*)**

- **A coarse, branched grass, growing wild in damp waste places, 1 to 6 feet tall. Leaves are long, pointed, broad and heart-shaped at the base, 4 to 16 inches length.**

- **Flowers are white, papery, borne on leaf axils, 1 to 4 inches long.**

- **Shiny, green, grey, black and white, hard, teardrop-shaped seeds are located at the tip of the flower stem.**

LEAD TREE

—Leucaena glauca

Ēkoa, Haole or Flase Koa, Wild Tamarind

- (Synonym: L. leucocephala by authors)

- Pea Family (*Fabaceae*)

- A common roadside and waste land shrub. Leaves are up to 12 inches long, having numerous, oblong, small leaflets.

- Flowers are yellowish white, round, about 1 inch in diameter.

- Seed pods are brown, hang in clusers, about 6 inches long, containing many small, dark brown, oval seeds.

MACADAMIA

—*Macadamia integrifolia*

Makekomia, Queensland Nut

- Silky Oak Family (*Proteaceae*)

- A medium-sized, fast-growing tree. Leaves are dark green, wavy, oblong with distant, prickles along the side.

- Flowers are whitish, about 7 inches long, tasseled.

- The nuts are brown, about 1 inch in diameter, enclosed inside a leathery, two-valved case which splits open when mature.

MADAGASCAR OLIVE
—*Noronhia emarginata*
'Oliwa Makakakeka

- Olive Family (*Oleaceae*)

- A small evergreen, tree. Leaves are shiny, oval, paired, about 6 inches long.

- Flowers are small, yellow, fragrant, four-parted, grows in clusters at leaf axils.

- Fruits are green to purplish when mature, 1 inch diameter, containing one large cream-colored, teardrop shaped seed.

MGAMBO

—*Majidea Zanquebarica*
Hua Weleweka, Velvet Seed

- Soapberry Family (*Sapindaceae*)

- A small tree. Leaves are alternate, simple, pinnately compound.

- Flowers are greenish-yellow with a touch of reddish in the center, small, in clusters on branch ends.

- The red seed pods, with 3 carpels, split open when mature, contains three, small, grey fuzzy seeds.

MONKEY POD

—*Samanea saman*
ʻŌhai, Rain Tree

- Pea Family (*Fabaceae*)

- A favorite shade, canopy shape tree, up to 80 feet or more. Leaves are compound, consisting of four to eight pairs of pinnae, each pinna of three to eight pairs of oblong leaflets, 1 to 2 inches long.

- Flowers are whitish-pink, in tufted heads, long pink stamens, about 2 inches in diameter.

- Pods are dark brown, about 7 inches in length, which do not open, containing small, oval, brown seeds around a sticky pulp.

OCHROSIA

—Ochrosia elliptica

Wahine-O-Ka-Hale (Lady-Of-The-House), Lady-Of-The Night, Pokosola

- Periwinkle Family (*Apocynaceae*)

- A small tree, known for its ornamental fruits. Leaves are oval, shiny, to 6 inches long, arranged in pairs.

- Flowers are small, cream-colored, fragrant, develops in clusters at or near branch ends.

- Fruits are bright red, oval, pointed drupes, 1 to 2 inches long, with a white, dry pulp, surrounding one large seed.

ORCHID TREE (HONG KONG)
—Bauhinia blakeana
La'au 'Okika, St. Thomas Tree, Pink Bauhinia

- Pea Family (*Fabaceae*)

- A small, beautiful, flowering tree, to about 20 feet tall. Leaves have double lobes, prominent veins radiate from the base.

- Flowers are rose-purple, fragrant, resembles an orchid blossom. However, it is not related to the orchid family.

- The seed pods are dark brown, about 12 inches long, containing many round to oval, flat seeds.

Betel Nut Palm
—*Areca catechu*
Nioi-pekela, Areca Palm

- Palm Family (*Arecaceae*)

- A palm tree, up to 100 feet tall, dark grey, ringed, non-swollen trunk. Leaves are 4 feet long or longer, the lowest one or two leaves usually drooping. The leaf divisions are 1 to 2 feet long.

- Flowers appear from under the leaf sheaths at the top of the trunk, yellowish white, about 1/3 inch long, fragrant.

- Mature fruits are orange or red, egg-shaped, up to 2-1/2 inches long, having a fibrous husk, containing a fleshy covering, around a deeply channeled seed.

BLEEDING HEART PALM
—*Veitchia joannis*
Hōʻeha-Puʻuwai, Niusawa Palm

- Palm Family (*Arecaceae*)

- A palm tree, about 30 feet high. Leaves are about 7 feet long, leaf divisions are 1 to 2 feet long, non-drooping leaves.

- Flowers are yellowish-white, about 1 inch long.

- Fruits are bright red, about 2 inches long, having a fibrous husk, containing a fleshy covering, around one large seed with a network of shallow lines, having a distinct scar down one side.

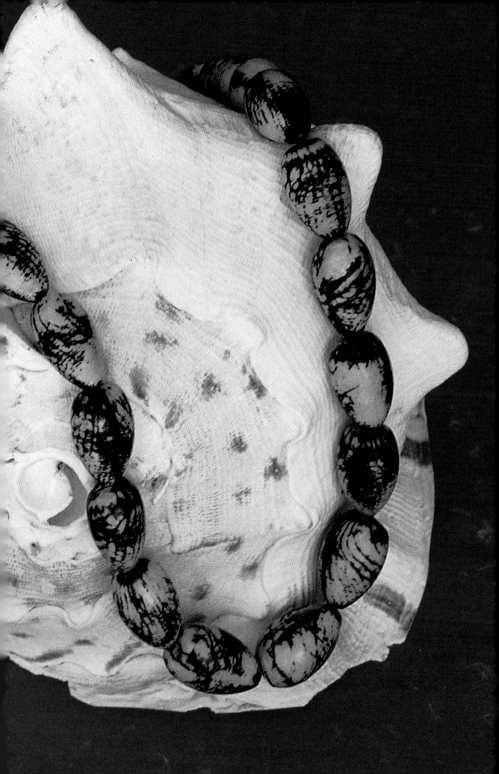

BURI PALM

—Polyandroccos caudescens
Pāma Pīlali (Wax Palm)

- Palm Family (*Arecaceae*)

- A medium, palm tree, with
  trunk up to 20 feet high,
  about 12 inches wide,
  bearing a large crown with
  stiff leaves 9 to 12 feet long,
  with about 150 sword-shaped leaflets.

- Flowers are yellowish, cascading downward on a long spike.

- Mature fruits are greenish-yellow, oval with a flattened
  base, about 1-1/2 inches long, having a fibrous husk,
  containing a fleshy covering, around an ovoid seed,
  having 3 pores at one end.

Chinese Fan Palm
—*Livistona chinensis*
Pāma Pe'ahi Kina, Fountain Palm

- Palm Family (*Arecaceae*)

- A fan palm tree with a dark trunk. Leaves are fan shaped, usually wind damaged.

- Flowers are small, yellowish, borne on sprays among the leaves, at a 45 degree angle.

- Fruits are about 3/4 inch long, bluish in color, containing one, oval seed.

COCONUT PALM
—*cocos nucifera*
Niu, Coco Palm

- Palm Family (*Arecaceae*)

- A palm tree with slender, seldom straight, ringed trunk, up to 100 feet tall.

- Leaves are flat, about 6 to 18 feet long, with long smooth fibrous-based stems, and numerous narrow leaflets 1 to 3 feet long, in a spreading cluster.

- Flowers are yellowish, in a branched cluster, many male flowers are on the long branches, while the female flowers are at the base of the branch.

- The mature fruits are green, yellowish to brown, about 12 inches long, triangular in cross section, having a thick fibrous husk, covering a roundish, hard nut, having 3 pores at one end.

Cohune Nut Palm

—Orbigyna cohune

Pāma Kūhiō, Kuhio Palm

- Palm Family (*Arecaceae*)

- A grand palm tree with a straight, smooth, grey, ringed trunk, about 50 feet tall.

- Leaves are dark green, plumelike, shooting about as high as the length of the trunk.

- Flowers are yellow, in spiral clusters, up to 6 feet long, emerging from a stiff, pink-lined sheath from between the leaves.

- Mature fruits are brown, ovoid, beaked, about 2 inches long, containing an oval nut, resembling a small coconut, having 3 pores at one end.

GRU GRU PALM
—*Acrocomia ierensis*
Pāma Hulu (Feather Palm)

- Palm Family (*Arecaceae*)

- A medium size palm tree, armed with spines 1 to 6 inches long on trunk and leaves. The leaflets are numerous, long, and narrow. The leaf stems are hairy and spiny.

- Flowers are on a large, long, hanging cluster. Female flowers are borne near the base of the branches, below the male flowers.

- The mature fruits are round, about 1 inch diameter, containing a one-seeded stone marked with three pores evenly divided on sides.

Lei from the collection of Patricia K. McGuire

LATAN (BLUE) PALM

—Latania loddigesii mart.

Pāma Lakana Polū, Blue Latan, Fan Palm

- **Palm Family (*Arecaceae*)**

- A fan palm up to 50 feet, slow growing, with a sturdy trunk marked with rings. Leaves are bluish, stiff, 3 to 5 feet long.

- Male and female flower spikes are borne on separate trees, up to 5 feet long, shorter with fewer branches on female trees.

- Mature fruits are green or yellowish green, oval, about 2 inches long, containing usually 3, teardrop-shaped, curved seeds.

Manila Palm

—*Veitchia merrillii* (formerly *Adonidia merrillii*)
Pāma Manila, Merrill Palm

- Palm Family (*Arecaceae*)

- A short palm tree, up to about 15 feet high, resembling a betelnut palm, having a shorter, thicker trunk, which may have a 10 inch diameter base. Leaves arch gracefully about 6 feet long, leaflets are close-set.

- Flowers are small, yellowish white, about 3/4 inch in diameter. The upper branches bear all male flowers, while the lower branches bear male and female flowers.

- Mature fruits are bright red, oval, about 1-1/4 inches long, having a slight fibrous husk, covering one, oval seed, marked with a network of lines, deeply channeled.

OIL PALM
—*Elaeis guineensis*
Pāma 'Aila, Gorilla Palm

- **Palm Family (*Arecaceae*)**

- **A slow growing palm tree with it's trunk covered with the remaining ends of old leaf stems.**

- **Leaves are wide, arching, up to about 15 feet, with many leaflets. The lowest leaflets are long thorns, which leads to shorter thorns on the edges of the stems.**

- **Male and female flowers develop on separate spikes, each branch ending with a thorn.**

- **Female flower spikes are about 12 inches long, larger than the cylindrical male spikes.**

- **Fruits are reddish to golden brown, ovoid, about 1-1/4 inches long, having a slight fibrous husk, mainly one-seeded, blackish, with 3 pores at one end.**

PRITCHARDIAS PALM

—*Pritchardia martii*

Loulu-Hiwa

- Palm Family (*Arecaceae*)

- A palm native to Hawaii, about 10 to 15 feet high, has a thick, ringed trunk. Leaves are fan-shaped, to 3 feet long, felted on the under side.

- Flowers are yellow, clustered, on spikes about 12 to18 inches long.

- Fruits are green to purplish black, ovoid, 1-1/2 inches long, having a fibrous husk, containing one, thin-shelled nut.

Queen Palm
—*Syagrus romanzoffiana*
(formerly *Arecastrum romanzoffianum* and *Cocos plumosa, Cocos romanzoffiana*)
Nui Keko (Monkey Nut), Feathery Coconut

- Palm Family (*Arecaceae*)

- An ornamental palm tree, 30 to 60 feet high, has a slender, straight, grey, ringed trunk.

- Leaves are bright green, wide arching, plumelike, curving downward, 10 to 15 feet long.

- Flowers are yellow, in a cluster, which hangs down from among the lower leaves, 3 to 6 feet long.

- The mature fruits are yellowish-orange, ovoid, about 1 inch long, containing a pulpy fiber, surrounding a nut, having 3 pores at one end.

PANDANUS

—*Pandanus Odoratissimus*

Hala, Screw Pine, Walking Tree, Pineapple Tree

- Screw Pine Family
  (*Pandanaceae*)

- A low tree, wide-branched,
  up to about 20 feet high,
  ringed trunk and branches,
  native to Hawaii. Leaves
  are about 3 feet long,
  narrow, sharp-pointed,
  and spirally arranged at
  branch ends.

- Male flower spikes (hinano) are about 12 inches long,
  fragrant, having white, pointed bracts, covering small
  yellow staminate flowers.

- Fruits are borne on female trees, yellowish when ripe,
  ovoid, about 8 inches diameter, resembles a pineapple,
  having about 50, wedge-shaped, yellow to red drupes,
  about 2 inches long, each with 4 to12 seed cells.

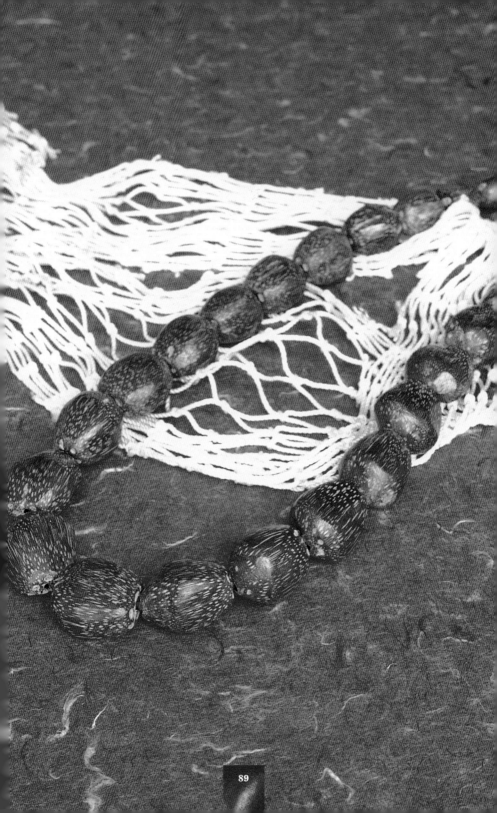

POGADA

—Mimusops elengi

Keli Kepania, Spanish Cherry, Elengi

- Sapodilla Family (*Sapotaceae*)

- An evergreen tree with inconspicuous milky sap. Leaves are dark green, smooth, oval, wavy-edged, 2 to 6 inches long.

- Flowers are white, about 1/2 inch long, fragrant, developing 2 to 6 in clusters on leaf axils.

- Fruits are, green to orange, ovoid, about 1 inch long, containing yellow pulp, surrounding one, flat, brown seed.

POINCIANA (DWARF)
—*Caesalpina pulcherrima*
'Ōha'i-Ali'i, Pride of Barbados

- (Synonym: Poinciana pulcherrima by authors)

- Pea Family (*Fabaceae*)

- A small tree or shrub, about 9 to15 feet high. Leaves are up to 12 inches long, divided into many leaflets, about 3/4 inch long.

- Flowers are bright red with yellow, about 1 inch long, in clusters, no fragrance.

- Seed pods are brown, about 4 inches long, curls open, containing about 6 to 8 seeds.

Lei from the collection of Louis Ko Ohana

POINCIANA (ROYAL)

—Delonix regia

'Ōha'i-'Ula, 'Ohai, 'Ula, Royal Flame, Flamboyant Tree, Flame Tree

- Pea Family (*Fabaceae*)

- A favorite flowering tree, known for the bright color when in bloom, branches look as if pulled down by the heavy pods, up to 40 feet tall. Leaves are fern-like, doubly compound, with small leaflets.

- Flowers are bright red, having five petals, one of the petals are white with the others red, while one of the petals are yellow with the others orange, about 2 inches long.

- The seed pods are brown, heavy, about 10 to 18 inches long, containing many long, greenish-brown seeds.

PORTIA

—*Thespesia populnea*

Milo

- **Mallow Family (*Malvaceae*)**

- **A popular shade tree, rarely up to 40 feet tall, trunk up to 24 inches in diameter.**

- **Leaves are heart-shaped, glossy, about 3 to 5 inches in diameter.**

- **Fresh flowers are pale yellow with a purpleish center, fading to purplish pink, about 2 to 3 inches in diameter.**

- **Seed cases are round, woody, five-parted capsule, about 1 inch in diameter, containing many light brown, downy covered seeds.**

SANDALWOOD (RED)
—*Adenanthera pavonina*
'Ula'ula, Flase Wiliwili, Bead Tree

- Pea Family (*Fabaceae*)

- A slender tree, up to 25 feet tall, wide spreading branches, pale grey, smooth bark. Leaves are compound, having many 1 to 2 inches long, blunt leaflets.

- Flowers are small, yellow, fragrant, in clusters at branch ends.

- Mature seed pods twist open on trees, dropping bright red, round, 1/3 inch diameter seeds, known as "Circassian seeds."

SANDBOX

—Hura crepitans

Onepahu, Hura

- Spruge Family
  (*Euphorbiaceae*)

- A large, spiny tree with
  poisionous milky sap.
  Leaves are deciduous,
  ovate to heart-shaped,
  about 6 inches long.

- Flowers are red, clustered, cone-shaped, about
  2 inches long.

- The mature fruits are brown, about 3 inches wide,
  resembling a miniature pumpkin, which burst open
  dropping many crescent-shaped seeds, about 1-1/2
  inches long.

- The milky sap is toxic if digested.

SEA BEAN

—Mucuna gigantea

Kā'e'e, Kā'e'e'e

- **Pea Family (*Fabaceae*)**

- **A strong, large, woody vine, wild in wet lowland forest. Leaves are about 10 inches long, divided into three leaflets, about 6 inches long.**

- **Flowers are chartreuse, about 1 inch long, hanging in a cluster, about 5 inches long, with a long stem.**

- **Mature seed pods are dark brown, about 4 inches long, containing 1 to 4 brown seeds with black vein-like lines, about 1 inch wide, each seed has a black band around three-fourths of the side of the seed.**

SEA BEAN (SHEEP EYE)
—*Mucuna urens*
Maka Hipa, Cow-itch Plant, Beach Bean

Photo courtesy of Native Habitat Ethnobotanicals

- **Pea Family (*Fabaceae*)**

- **A vine, up to 30 feet long, growing wild on mountain slopes and in valleys. Leaves are broad, ovate, having three leaflets, 2 to 5 inches long.**

Photo by Wayne P. Armstrong

- **Flowers are yellow and red, 2 inches long, hanging in a cluster at leaf ends.**

- **Seed pods are dark brown, thick, oblong, have stinging hairs which are dangerous to the skin and eyes, containing 1 to 2 round, 1 inch wide seeds, each seed has a black band around three-fourths of the side of the seed.**

SEA GRAPE

—*Coccoloba uvifera*
Waina Kai

- Buckwheat Family
  (*Polygonaceae*)

- A small to medium tree, planted for windbreaks near beaches, up to about 20 feet tall. Leaves are rounded, up to 8 inches diameter.

- Flowers are white, fragrant, in spikes about 6 inches long.

- Mature fruits are green to reddish purple, roundish-shape, 3/4 inch long, hang in clusters about 7 inches long, containing a light to medium brown, round seed capsule with 3 heart-shaped, brown, small seeds.

SOAPBERRY (HAWAIIAN)

—*Sapindus saponaria*
Mānele, a'e, Soap Seed

- Soapberry Family
  (*Sapindaceae*)

- A native tree to Hawaii and
  tropical America, up to 80
  feet high, flaky-barked trunk.
  Leaves are compound, light
  green, 2 to 5 inches long,
  having 4 to 12 paired,
  pointed leaves.

- Flowers are chartreuse, five-parted, at branch ends.

- Fruits are browinsh yellow, shiny, round, having a sticky
  sap, covering a black, shiny, round seed, 1/2 inch diameter.

SOAPBERRY (O'AHU)

—*Sapindus oahuensis*

Āulu, Kaulu or Lonomea, Man of the House

Photo by George K. Linney

- Soapberry Family
  (*Sapindaceae*)

- A native tree up to 60
  feet high, whitish
  trunk, in dry areas.
  Leaves are simple,
  ovate, deep green, smooth,
  about 3 to10 inches long.

- The flowers are small, whitish brown, 7 to 8 protruding
  stamens, in clusters on branch ends.

- The mature fruits are yellowish brown, oblong, about
  1-1/4 inches long, containing an oblong, groved, black seed.

TAMARIND

—*Tamarindus indica*
Wi-'awa'awa

- Pea Family (*Fabaceae*)

- A slow growing, evergren, shade tree, having spreading branches, up to about 80 feet tall. Leaves are graceful, feathery, having 10 to 20 pairs of 1/2 inch long leaflets.

- Flowers are small, red and yellow, having 3 petals.

- Seed pods are brown, 1 to 6 inches long, having a sticky brown pulp, surrounding brown, roundish, flat seeds.

Wood Rose

—Operculina tuberosa

Pili-Kai

- (Synonym: Ipomoea tuberosa by authors)

- Morning-Glory Family (*Convolvulaceae*)

- A smooth, perennial vine. Leaves are 5 to 7 lobed, up to 8 inches in diameter.

- Flowers are yellow, about 2 inches long, resembling a morning glory blossom.

- Fruiting capsules are brown, stiff, flower-shaped, containing 1 to 4, black, downy covered seeds.

Lei from the collection of Louis Ko Ohana

TOXIC SEEDS

Common Name	Scientific Name	Symptoms
Be-still	Thevetia puruviana	Whole plant very toxic
Black-Eyed Susan	Arbus precatorius	Raw seeds highly toxic if eaten or enters skin through a cut
Canavalia	Canavalia cathartica	Seeds toxic if eaten in quantity
Candlenut	Aleurites moluccana	Raw seeds physic is eaten
Coral Tree	Erythrina varigata indica	Seeds toxic with HCN if eaten in quantity
Cycad-Sago Palm	Cycas circinalis	Raw seeds very toxic if eaten
Jack In The Box	Hernandia ovigera	Seed contents may irritate skin
Java Olive	Sterculia foetida	Hair around seed may irritate skin
Macadamia	Macadamia integrifolia	Leaves and nut shell contains HCN if eaten in quantity
Ochrosia	Ochrosia elliptica	Sap toxic
Sandalwood (Red)	Adenanthera pavonina	Raw seeds toxic if eaten
Sandbox	Hura crepitans	Sap of tree toxic
Soapberry	Sapindus saponaria	Leaves and fruits toxic if eaten

HCN = Hydrocyanic Acid-Cyanide

Lei from the collection of
'Ano'ano namea hana lima ō Hālawa

BIBLIOGRAPHY

Austin, D. F. 1998 *Poisonous Plants of Southern Florida*. Published on WWW at http://www.fau.edu/divdept/science/envsci/poison-pl.html.

Coombes, Allen J. *Dictionary of Plant Names*. Portland, Oregon: Timber Press, 1985.

Graf, Alfred Byrd. *Tropica Color Cycllopedia of Exotic Plants and Trees; for Warm Regions—Horticultures, in Cool Climate The Summer Garden or Sheltered Indoors, Second Edition, Revised and Enlarged*. East Rutherford, NJ: Roehrs Company, 1991.

McCurrach, James C. *Palms of the World*. New York: Harper and Brothers, 1980.

McDonald, Marie A. *Ka Lei: The Leis of Hawaii*. Honolulu: Press Pacifica, 1989.

Neal, Marie C. *In Gardens of Hawaii*. Honolulu: Bishop Museum Press, 1965.

Pukui, Mary Kawena, and Elbert, Samuel H. *Hawaiian Dictionary, Revised and Enlarged Edition*. Honolulu: University of Hawaii Press, 1986.

Smith, A. W. *A Gardener's Dictionary of Plant Names*. New York: St. Martin's Press, 1972.

Wagner, Warren L., Herbst, Derral R., and Sohmer, S. H. *Manual of the Flowering Plants of Hawaii, Volume I & II*. Honolulu: University of Hawaii Press, Bishop Museum Press, 1990.

Whistler, Arthur W. *Flowers of the Pacific Island Seashore*. Hawaii: Isle Botanica, 1992.